ELIZABETHAN

VI

JONATHAN LOVEJOY

Jonathan Lovejoy

ELIZABETHAN

The Complete Poems of Elizabeth Peele

Volume VI

Jonathan Lovejoy

Armageddon Publishing

Cover: *After the Bath,* 1875
William Adolphe Bouguereau (1825-1905)

ISBN-10: 0692319212
ISBN-13: 978-0692319215

For every Elizabeth

Introduction

Carmen Angelina Coletti (Elizabeth Peele) was perhaps the greatest composer who ever lived. After her death, studies of her music revealed a body of work—almost exclusively instrumental—of such beauty and power as to defy description. Even so, her lifelong reclusiveness rendered them obsolete to the world, and these musical treasures may remain apart from public view forever.

Even those few who heard her original scores did so in quiet apprehension, that this beautiful widow—lost somewhere deep in North Carolina farming country—brought forth music as completely ingenious as any ever written before. The sounds of greatness flowing from this woman's piano, surely this is not meant to be! For what purpose can she truly serve as a neoclassical composer in a jaded modern world, except as a curiosity and eventually, a fountain of eternal exploitation?

But while music did serve as a profession for her since she was twelve—her only wage being a sound mind and spirit—there was still another expression, both private and unintentional, equally meant for her eyes only. Gathered posthumously, so few of these "assemblies" can be called unique or special, and likely cannot set her apart from any other lonely poet in the world. But still they live on, as a glimpse into the mind of a musical genius and abused woman of Faith. Written parallel to her music over the years—with no striving for greatness or immortality—these poetic trifles, ironically, may be the only compositions of hers the world will ever hear.

Jonathan Lovejoy

ELIZABETHAN

or

"The Assemblies"

Volume VI

Jonathan Lovejoy

Such is the grandest music among us—

Poets…

Such are the wildest thoughts among us—

Composers…

The Book of Suzanne

155th Assembly

753

The evil voice is very strong

Stings as the mighty Bee

Truth should reveal itself in love

For all the world to see

The voice of good is very strong

Dispels the nerve to flee

Kindness is the Healing Stream

That every word should be

754

Crimson, white and midnight fall
From light down to the floor
Shadows creep below the azure wave
Where Armageddon reigns—forevermore

755

He beckoned from inside the wall

Awake—arise! Accept thy call

Hold the Death Stroke at bay with rest—

Debilitating—

756

I have no right to boast—

Of any accomplishment
We are only a product—
Of what is meant to be

One in a sea—
Of those with the same ability
But whom God allows to find a treasure,
In the field of those who have sought to find it

What is there to boast of
When I was only where he predestined me to be!
 All gifts, every gift
Is from the Almighty God

All success is his to give
Or to take away just the same
These gifts are of the heart
And the mind—
And the body

Jonathan Lovejoy

To allow us to fulfill our Destiny

Which is not of ourselves—

But of God

156th Assembly

757

Colors of genius threaten to loom

Painted stupidity

Seeking to hide the truth in foolishness

With intrepidity

Almost a prisoner of evil

Inside the upper room

By a woman bound in lustful vengeance

And prophecies of doom

Send love and a great arranger

To Chambers of Foxworth Hall

The Children are in danger

Without knowing it at all

758

Symbols of woman to woman

Flashed on every screen

The newest modern perversion

Waiting to be seen

759

She is the kind of woman

Who shuts other women down

Simply by walking into a room

The room fills with quiet prayers that she is nice

For if she is not—

She will affect a chip off their self-esteem A wound as painful

As that of the flesh itself

760

Outside the Halls of Learning

Across the Great Lawn

In a hurry to escape the perils of goodwill—

At the hands of other people

In grieving for a time without fear

Nor the horror of pain and suffering

Pain caused by brutality—

At the hands of other people

As part of the Curse of Man

From here to East of Eden

Men, women and children are burdened by violence—

From the hands of other people

Jonathan Lovejoy

157th Assembly

761

*F*our is a number of completion
Given for the world to know
Gospels, winds, seasons, horseman
Divine consequences to show

762

Black eyed peas are on the brain
A rhythm in desperate skill
Recipes of seasoned melody
With time and money to kill

Professor, Indian, Radical, Beauty
Snaked in a whirling verve
Drunk on the wine of adulation
Par for what course they deserve

Black eyed peas are on the brain
Rhymes of seasoned perfection
Songs prepared in Last Day's Kitchen
A natural end time selection

Jonathan Lovejoy

763

In the Halls of Learning, a ghost appears

Staring into my soul

Confounding me in the form of woman

Fires from the heart of Sheoul

764

I gather muses from the shelf

Quietly in the night

What eight legged visitor is this

Shocking my soul to fright!

Falling, drifting to the carpet floor

Oil to a wayward spark!

Bent to carry my solace away—

Hiding in the dark

Jonathan Lovejoy

158th Assembly

765

She shines a light upon the Hill

For every heart to see

Amherst East—the Grieving Hall

Too far away from me

To know her is *"to know her less*

The nearer her they get"

Verses shrouded in Lavender

With ashen gray regret

Goals at rest lie unattained

Beyond where I can see

Thy light shines bright upon the Hill

Draw me near unto thee!

766

Nature and human nature are intertwined

Joined by the same curse of God

And so, the Earth suffers—

As do we

For the two of them, there is beauty

Shades of perfection

But burdened by the shadows of Eden

And Gethsemane

Jonathan Lovejoy

767

Venomous serpents roam about

Striking the skin to blood

Leaving the victim in awe of transpiry

Crawling back through the mud

False signs and wonders all around

Permeating the air

Flailing the heart and mind adrift

With sadness and despair

Subtle serpents roam about

Where bufferflies should be

Corrupting the Earth with fear and poison

With cordiality

768

Mercury rising—
Along the plane of the ecliptic
Upon wings of a fiery trip
Hidden from our view

Venus rising—
Along the plane of the ecliptic
The brightest star in the second heaven
In the morning and evening day

Earth rising—
Along the plane of the ecliptic
Shining colors of a deep blue sea
Brushed by silken clouds of white

Mars rising—
Along the plane of the ecliptic
Glowing as a red star
A desert colored in blood

Jupiter rising—
Along the plane of the ecliptic
Banded color storms of mystery
Raging in the cold

Saturn rising—
Along the plane of the ecliptic
Shaded by the Amber Harvest
In the beauty of the ring

Uranus rising—
Along the plane of the ecliptic
Clouds tinted by Jade snow
Devoured by the cold

Neptune rising—
Along the plane of the ecliptic
A blue light too far away to see
Lost in perpetual winter

Pluto rising—
Along the plane of the ecliptic
Darkness frozen in the centuries
On the edge of space and time

159th Assembly

769

Demons masquerade as children
In the light of the brightest moon
While the Lie appears in nighttime shadow
Burning in the sky

Debra Anne is greater, they say
Bow thy song to she
Under the light of the brightest moon
Beneath the Great Sequoia Tree

770

The world renown gathers together

To toss silliness in the air

Ignoring the underprivileged in their hearts

A burden of happiness to bear

Those who are mocked with unmerciful derision

With no more dignity to spare

Look to Heaven for a relief from pain

A cloak of righteousness to wear

The world renown gathers together

Pretending that they care

Throwing money and silliness around

With monumental despair

771

Life was love and love is lost

Forever and again
Now there is hope for the final day
And rain upon my grave

I'll find my happiness through the door
Down Cemetery Way
To leave the burden of life behind
For others to endure

772

Return to thy prison—Dead One!

In your upper room

Kiss Living Death on her rosy cheek

Embrace her desire to own

Seek not to escape thy coffin of birth

Curse this desire to roam

Rest easy while the feeling burns your flesh

Let your casket be your happy home!

Jonathan Lovejoy

160th Assembly

773

Choose the path closest to your heart
To not be led astray
Though others may sabotage your method
Push 'til your dying day

Red stone, Blue stone, Gold stone, Green
Pick what your soul will need
The wrong one makes the heart regret
Colors chosen in greed

Searching through the ancient caves
We came upon the stone
The Statue God said *"choose wisely"*
"Then make your choices known"

Foolishly, I took the Gold
A choice I did not mean
I tucked the richest stone away
Wishing that it was Green

Elizabethan VI

To my companions—I begged— *"Where is the stone?"*
The one I need to get?
I took the wrong one from the Cave...
I'm sickened with regret!

Marguerite emerged from the beneath the Earth
Holding my stone in awe
The shining emerald closest to my heart
Clutched in her thieving claw

In agony, I begged her for the stone
And any price to pay
Knowing I have to persist with her
Until my dying day

774

A teenager was attacked by his father
In the name of discipline itself
The father insisted on hitting him
With plyboard as thick as a shelf

Leave me alone, the boy cried
You'll be sorry if you don't
One day I'll bash your skull in
Please don't think that I won't

775

The Moon shines over the west

In glory from above

People running to and fro—

In the shadows below

Days when the sky was blue

Nights beneath the stars

Signs and wonders stroll the fields

Where did the lilies go?

776

He woke up with a sudden start
In the middle of the night
Pushing his feet into the dark
Feeling an awful fright!

He pushed his foot toward empty space
Moving above a chair
Lightning struck his brain to sparks—
Something was sitting there

161st Assembly

777

In their hiding Mansion Northwest

Abiding in the rain

Where Heaven bestows peace and harmony

Wealth and riches to gain

778

*C*uriosity killed the prodigal son
Grieving his poor mother

Plunging his father to prosaic despair
Verses like no other

In the Land of the Free and the home of the brave
Violence fills the street
No one is safe when they leave their home
From anyone they meet

779

On a stroll through the atramental forest
Under trees grown to infinity
A prehistoric creature appears in warning
To usher us to safety

Beauty calls men to fore
To conduct themselves lasciviously
At the edge of the atramental forest
Before the second coming

Beasts are heard from among the trees
From deep inside the dark'ned woods
Prompting a climb to the top of the Hill
Where the landscape can be seen

From deep within the Jade Forest
A white machine rolls to fore
Spreading fear in no consequence
Among the Children of the Woods

780

The fiery clown bangs the basement door

Shrieking to be set free

Promising himself that the world would pay

Most inevitably

Jonathan Lovejoy

162nd Assembly

781

Asking those who are in the know

Have I wasted my time

They mimmeled and mumbled—hemmed and hawed

Wisdom not worth a dime

"Answer me," I said, "I'm in the dark!"

 "Am I wasting my time?"

Crushed by the same cryptic nonsense from them—

Clarity—is the crime!

782

Shrubs need not be jealous of trees

Whispering in the wind

Let them endeavor to reach the sky

Struggling until the end

Rising to the height of glory

For every one to see

Struck by lightning in a storm—

Most unavoidably

783

Golden bands of time—

Chosen to tick away

In places of inferiority

Where mothers seek to rise

Unclothed—among the learned ones

Who peppered in the mill

One with glasses, one whose not—

Seeking to destroy

784

Rides yield a fruitless melody—
From the bottom to the top
Rolling the nightime evergreen
Then to a sudden halt

Jonathan Lovejoy

785

I should like to avoid a boggy acre

Or even an ear of corn

To see the landscape unfettered

Where the sun will rise

Amherst Lake shall call to fore

Purpose under the sun

I choose to plow the public fields

Under the cloak of night

163rd Assembly

786

Melodies are better in the house

Than scattered to the winds

Rolling empty streets in the dark

Like a blue spay-veen fool

A glimpse of "The Epic" in the clouds

On the eve of a rain

Embarking the black chariot to nowhere

 Forward and back again

787

Ahole devouring in space

Where every eye can see

Sin burning the fabric of time

Where Earth men choose to be

The burn repairs along the timeline

Fair maidens live to tell

When comets blaze the eastern sky

With no new home to dwell

Iron Pyrites come and go Fashion slaves play the fool

Never mind that souls might go to Perdition

 Who clipped the Golden Rule

Back and forth and to and fro

Life is all the same

Running to avoid the responsibility

Of Armageddon's Flame

788

She sees as places they are shattered
These are groups with a "C" on
Made in loops the people gather
Displayed on troops with a "B"on

This one hearkens from somewhere still
A drift tide over the barn
Like sun drenched air on a balmy day
Looking for no more weaves to darn

The flower pretties know where its at
Crying in the Learning Hall
They want the tears to be kept in flow
'Til they reach their final call

789

The Passion of the Christ will let us know

What hour of the day has come

Telling us where to put our minds

For the beating of the kettledrum

"I am very wise," he said

"I don't need your God"

The flowering trees will be blowing in the Wind

With neither a wink nor a nod

164th Assembly

790

The Movie Man wept silently forward
No one had besieged him
Terrified by the monsters brought to life
No one had believed him

The Movie Man's dynasty stayed in tact
When tripods came to Earth
Making the rest of them run for cover
By predestiny's Growth and Girth

Lulled by movies that have come before
Of various degree
Put in their place by the power of God
And aliens to see

Their sanity will be commandeered
By what he seeks to do
The scariest tale that was ever told
In summer's vista view

Elizabethan VI

Death and Fire all around

Brass and basses drumming

Soaked by the tripods invading Earth—

On the eve of His Second Coming

791

*W*henceforth didst thou genius fly?

What carries it aloft?

Over the dangerous, treacherous journey

To its impossible destination

These are winds of opportunity

Flowing the timeline, in the lives of a blessed few

Opportunity flows in the Winds of Time—

To carry us aloft

792

Pencil scribbled on the black page

Has no secrets to reveal

Wives dressed for the world stage

Have no secrets to conceal

793

They say no quarter will be given

What is it that they mean?
Is it concerning the quality of mercy

With nothing in between?

Lucky faces in the fighting corps
 In grieving for a time
When no prayers are needed to stay alive

In battlefields of war

Even in the heart of battle
Depravities remain
Those lucky in lasciviousness
And carnal sins to gain

Those who don't know invade the peace
Screaming from down below
Ascending the stairs in ignorance
And pains of life to show

Elizabethan VI

Those from the past are asked to leave

In sorrow of desire

Told to never again return

To Socrates on fire

Jonathan Lovejoy

165th Assembly

794

Losers cross the beaten path

Grieving for a fight

Drunken on the wine of hate they cause

Suffering in their plight

As the Word Man waits for another calling

Played in the key of "C"

A major happening along the timeline

 In keyboard harmony

Drawn by the cry of modulation

A wooded path is shown

Set for knowledge upon the keyboard

Previously unknown

795

Jade Silk will pass the test
In the armament of time
Cutting with a diamond sword
Crafted by an angel

Her trip through life--rife with danger
In days where strife shall rule
Knowing what the new dead sea scroll has warned
 She slices with her blade

The assassin's name is Jade Silk
Born of man and woman
Seeking to cut with her diamond blade
Looking for souls to kill

Beneath the light of the brightest Moon
Flies a spirit in green
With the blood of a man's wife on her sword
Fading into the night

796

A duo of masculine beauty

Golden melodies to sing

Languished in the heart of hatred

Until the end of time

Called to mimic the songbirds

Heaped in fortune and fame

Until the world saw behind the curtain

Uncovering their shame

One who writhes in obscurity

One in the torment of death

Both to carry 'til the end of time

The burden of their blame

797

There are feelings in space—answers to the lover's whim

Someone has to see them

This is the way of their little world

No one tries to be them

They spoke in matters of the heart

So many years ago

The answers are in a little black dress

That she designed for show

798

One must bear the weight of his ship

Turning in the wind

The smell of ice is in the air

All set to buck the trend

She died upon her maiden voyage

Luxury split in two

Now the ocean is a watery grave

With burying to do

166th Assembly

799

Alogna Allini failed the test

In the adoration of slavery

Captivity in dreams and visions

On the road to nowhere

The depth of cunning is revealed

But to no avail

As the orchestra plays strands of genius

 Until the end of time

Sliding the flow of history

Along the current of Debra Anne

Who knows all things work together for good

To them who love God

Alogna Allini passed the test

In the abolition of slavery

While the ancestry rests in ignorance

Under Bel Canto

800

Thaéon Massét appears in a lie

From ashen gray regret
When storms coalesce a dark'ned sky
A fallen angel slips by and bye
Guile and deceit clips the evil eye…
In earthen silhouette

The Devil conjures a sabotage
With hopes to burn the page
Satan sends the demon entourage
Dispatched in a nightmare camouflage
They commence the worldwide war barrage…
To end the present age

801

A great roaring, lumbering beast

Runs from in the woods

Covered in white from head to toe

Raging through the snow

802

"Just give us the money, dude!" they said

Then the robbers showed their gun

Smiling like two Cheshire cats

As though they were having fun

The man knew he didn't have a dime

Nor a single penny to give

So he closed his eyes and thought of pain

And how long he had left to live

Jonathan Lovejoy

167th Assembly

803

Have you enjoyed the trip to bountiful?

Along the path—

To where your husband died?

804

Echoes of a past life resound

Given before my time

A scene played out in the darkness of pain

With violence as the crime

Jonathan Lovejoy

805

*F*oolish attempts at bravery

Bring threats to life and limb—

806

*R*olling the ancestry to nowhere
Predestined by the Fates
   On the eve of treasures lost and found

   A white chariot awaits

   God is divided into three

   And then these three are one

   The Father, the Son, the Holy Ghost

   No mystery--its done!

   One in unrequited life

   One in longing for sleep

   Both in search of Days of Heaven

   In a new house to keep

   Cruising the roads of prosperity

   Their spirits called to roam

   Lost in the nighttime infinity In grieving for a home

Jonathan Lovejoy

168th Assembly

807

Muddy waters cloud thy murderous bog
On the shores of hometown bliss
The privileged ones say "come hither"
Promising to show the way

The waters run with sparkling clarity
In the sun of the morning day
Until it is clouded from another source
From other waters unknown

The simple seeks to confound the wise
When the waters of the bog are drained
Relaxed in death defying claustrophobe
Lying in the mud

Authorites from the past appear
Lending credence to the mystery
The mystery of the sparkling waters
And the muddy bog therein

Elizabethan VI

The privileged walk the Earth in unfriendliness
Assured of their position
Whispering promises that will never keep
In the Palace of the Golden Hall

Even from the mouths of ancestry
Incongruities abound
Walking through the Forest of the Sparkling Water
Contaminated by the mud

Hope appears in ambiguity
On the Ring of the Golden Keys
Enticing themselves in mid-air
Glinting in the sun

In the Forest of the Sparkling Waters
In the cool of the morning day
Beneath the trees that stretch to infinity
On the eve of prosperity

All paths lead into the riverbed
And the banks of darkened clay
Fear resides primarily in the heart
And not the shadows of reality

Lions have formed in thine own eyes
To yield phantom teeth and claws
Crawl quickly through the underbrush!
Over the traveling rail!

The light means that something is coming through the woods
Hurry before it gets here!
In the Forest of the Sparkling Water
In the cool of the morning day

The House of Poverty is a house of change
From cerulean to alabaster
Floors of burnished oakwood
With no furniture to bear

But the room of memory has replenished itself
In the manner of its choosing
Every wall of white is blue again Above
the amber carpeted floor

In this hallowed hall of memory
Beyond the Forest of the Sparkling Water
The ancestry speaks of the Golden Key
And climbing every mountain

808

The North Wind blows an icy kiss
From somewhere atop the spinning Earth
With winter's warning in her voice
Whirling autumn leaves to their death

The South Wind blows a heated wave
From the center of the spinning Earth
With empty promises of rest and play
On the eve of the whirlwind

The East Wind blows a morning breeze
At the foot of the rising sun
Hearkening for those to awaken
To see Aurora vanish away

The West Wind blows an evening breeze
At the foot of the setting sun
Whispering in the evening day
Beneath the fall of night

809

Humanity should close its eyes and pray
To God, Christ and the Fates
On the eve of intergalactic war—
 Extermination waits

This shall remove hope from mankind—
Thermonuclear war
The consequences of his own actions
Until there is no more

Time on Earth is winding down
To devastation—and loss
Because men will fly planes into buildings
To get their point across

810

*C*louds of why roll in

Screaming for me to know

Why oh why, oh Lord—

Does eschatology have to show?

Jonathan Lovejoy

169th Assembly

811

The new corn grows green and beautiful

Underneath skies of gray

I run to the end of the rows I see

In this bereaving day

The ancestry warns of ill-advised trips

Fearful to some degree

While the cropfield stretches to infinity

Where my hometown used to be

812

*G*o home—

Go home and slam the door in my face

I'm not there anymore

So your anger will be ineffectual

Go home—

Slam the door in my face

See if I care—

Who does it hurt?

813

When a demon manifestation is in your home

Don't forget it

Don't leave it in the walls

To contaminate your life

When you move into a home

A place with filthy, dirty walls

That filth can be demonic

Left over energy from evil lives

The ones who lived there before

Demons of violence—

Drunkenness—

Illicit sex

Lying, stealing—

Adultery—

Pray and paint those demons away—

Until your new house is clean

814

The music man was that of legend
Living a life of peace
Until he was shot by an assassin's bullet
Looking for souls to kill

Irony makes the air hard to breathe
Like water in the sea
She said *"tell all the truth but tell it slant"*
For this very reason

There's no irony on the modern stage
Only a lust for fame Mediocrity is the calling card—
Sinfulness is the game

Jonathan Lovejoy

170th Assembly

Jonathan Lovejoy

815

I would like to say *"I heard a fly buzz when I died"*

But it was spoken first

By a genius who died a thousand deaths—

A Queen of Wicked Verse

A shaking, a quaking, a stirring

Underneath clouds of gray

The angel said "you have a decision to make"

And then he went away

In the turning of another day

A resurrected me

Elizabethan VI

816

The fire shown in his sunglasses
Until he took them off
Though he was as plain as a man could be
There was no need to scoff

Without effort, he drew the fire from the room
Flaming it on his hands
Then with hidden malice he looked at me
Ready to show his plans

He rubbed the fire over his shirtless body
Lighting his skin in flame
The fire burned without consuming him
And then we played his game

Glass vats of green and reddish liquid
Waiting off to the side
Magically changing colors back and forth
Just like a runaway bride

Storm music rolls the countryside

Two centuries before

For fools not knowing it will be heard

For two whole cent'ries more

817

There were no cities and states

In the early days of mankind

They walked and talked and hunted

According to their need

Then one day, trouble grew out of the ground

In the form of rock and brick

The first villages and towns appeared

The beginning of the end

Then later by Predestiny

Towns grew to their requisite sizes

For some—trouble was little and simple

For others—trouble was big and complex

And they were not always aware—

Of the serpent's crawl among the living

As he surveyed the dark'ned streets

With a forked tongue—

And a plan

Jonathan Lovejoy

818

Winded clocks—nighttime trips

What is it that we know?

A loser's life—is simply that

There's nowhere else to go

Blackbirds on the trail of life

Following every step

Lulu tells the whole story

No one will say a word

Take care along the way, traveler

Don't let hope be your guide

It will lead you to a muddy bog

The place where you belong

Elizabethan VI

Jonathan Lovejoy

171st Assembly

819

*B*e wary not to consign your treasures

You'll be seiged with regret
Let charity have another day
When you can pay the debt

Be generous in another form
One you can bear to pay
So that charity can renew itself
And faith can have its way

820

Icons are brought down to nothing
In the eyes of the Lord
Legends are turned to dying refuse
In the eyes of the Lord

Man's glory is nothing
Grand unto himself
The Glory of the Lord is your strength
While the wicked prosper

821

If I were dead, I would say nothing
To the souls among the living

I would watch them blow themselves to bits
With nary a passing thought

A world of no cities
No generosity
Only weeping and gnashing of teeth—
Under the ashe cloud

822

ake Mr. Edison at his word—
Genius is 99 percent perspiration
But *the other* part is more elusive
Being 99 percent imagination

Jonathan Lovejoy

823

At the edge of a mountain forest
In the company of a new fallen snow
I see above the dark'ned line of trees
The remains of the age in the sky

The lunar light is scattered—in orbit
Spreading out—from east to west
Dust and debris of another time
Another infinity

824

Make a descent into a basement if you dare

In a quiet house at night

Stay there until you know—beyond the shadow of a doubt

That you are not alone

There is no bravery beneath the Earth

Where demons live and breathe

Masquerading as souls of the dead

Gliding through the walls

Jonathan Lovejoy

825

I am content to live with ghosts

What harm can they do?
It is the living that must be feared
Rather than the dead

Gathered in the Hall of Worship
This prayer being to commerce—
Earth angels sit at the table in bare white feet
Looking over with disdain and ambiguity—

I am content to live with ghosts
What harm can they do?

A flood of new apprehension comes through the door
Causing anxiety
Swimming through the flood of accursed water
To the alter of worship

Placing the ticket on the counter—
 Incorrectly
Being told by demons of pitch
"You're a fool!"

Elizabethan VI

Mistakes are unforgivable
In the Money Palace
Their speech and mocking causes ire
Threatening to morph into murder—

Predestiny

Time among the living has ended
No longer aware of them
Content to be frightened by demons of the dead—
Rather than those of the living

826

Spinning, twirling, whirling about

Sinfulness has no bounds

Touching every gender, age and creed

Whose wickedness astounds

Lasciviousness touches all humanity

One way or another

Causing the child to look with wonder

As sin takes hold of its mother

Million dollar ambitions

Sabotaged early on

Quelled by jealousy and envy

Killed until its gone

173rd Assembly

Jonathan Lovejoy

827

Braving a fervent desire to roam—

From bottom to the top

Craving the fires of a home—

Where fear and pain will stop

The Road to Nowhere has begun

Among mountains and the hills

With foreboding to the setting sun

And the promise it fulfills

Colors fade until they die

In the aftermath of light

Stars twinkle in a summer sky—

On their journey through the night

828

Braving a fervent desire to roam—
From bottom to the top
Craving the fires of a home—
Where fear and pain will stop

The Road to Nowhere has begun
Among mountains and the hills
With foreboding to the setting sun
And the promise it fulfills

Colors fade until they die
In the aftermath of light
Stars twinkle in a summer sky—
On their journey through the night

829

I live to cause problems, she said
Between a man and his wife
No greater satisfaction there is
Than to cause turmoil and strife

A little harmless flirting
If done at just the time
Will throw a wrench in the marital works
As though he did the crime

While his wife stepped in the grocery place
 I took a devilish cue
Pressing against his body hard
For the pleasure that was due

I persuaded him to touch me
In a manner unlike before
Until my friends said, leave him alone—
You're acting like a whore!

830

There is apt to be a slaughter
Dead bodies all around
Humanity will tremble at the bone
When the trump of God shall sound

Fear will spread throughout the Earth
In the manner of a crimson vine
Creeping the heart of every soul—
As aliens bring the sign

Jonathan Lovejoy

174th Assembly

Jonathan Lovejoy

831

You pray that seven days will cease
For your suffering to last
This prayer flows across the weeks
Until seven years has passed

The mirror cracked when you were born
And shattered to the floor
Scattered shards at your mothers feet—
Good luck is out the door!

832

He says he is afraid of knocking

Accent on the tragic key

Wedding marches—they come a walkin'

Down to where the world can see

Tragic is as tragic does

No need to wish for a higher "c"

Emptiness has fouled aplenty

In the place where happiness used to be

Nowhere else is morbid truth

Seen as pleasure ought to reap

Unknown reasons echo the mind

Like sunken treasures of the deep

Jonathan Lovejoy

833

In the Great Competition Hall

Preordained failure waits—

By the light of the first crescent Moon

In grieving to be born

Old strategies cannot prevail

Over the preordained

As new strategies are corrupted as well

In Competition Hall

Those that are out are in

Those that are in are out

All seeking a declaration of victory

Over the preordained

834

Silence in the darkened hall
Crushed in expectation
Suddenly a light appears
To declare the victor

A less impressive ray of light Shines for the preordained
Drawing a chorus of oooh's and aaah's
From the astonished hoarde

The winner walks the pride of living
In unimpressive light
While the other learns what it is to be
A loser in this life

175th Assembly

Jonathan Lovejoy

836

Jody's eyes are still watching
From somewhere in the house
Eyes of ruby laser light
Blazing the fire of Hell

The human body cannot endure real fear
In such great quantities
When the physical limit is achieved
 Death is the last resort

Pointless, endless labour threatens
To bring a soul to naught
It appears that errors have been made
Concerning a future

'Twas a punishment from God
Designed to cause more pain
There were no divine declarations made
Or promises to keep
Faith is shaken to the bone

Elizabethan VI

'Til only doubt remains
With nothing more at all to lose
And all the more to gain

836

Libido is the death of some

A seething, raging beast

Circumstances by which they are—

Not sorry in the least

Female attire has come to naught

'Specially on TV

These last days are aflame of fire—

And sensuality

The Great White Cat is out of the bag

And she is dressed to kill

Devouring those from far and near—

With necromantic skill

837

People suffer because of sin

And deservedly so

Causing chastisement to fall from Heaven

Like poison flakes of snow

What pain is punishment for sin?

Remains a mystery

Correction drifts from God to all—

Because of history

838

Where pearls do languish in a row
To set the stage for pain
Do Cerulean eyes know the curse of Beauty?
Driving them all insane?

It storms from the blight of Adam's Clay
The cooling of the eve
Knowledge strolls the Garden in regret
Hoping for a reprieve

Truth must flourish in the shadows
Those with a blinder on
Will see her silhouette clutching me—
In lavender and Dawn

176th Assembly

Jonathan Lovejoy

839

I now have reason to go to sleep

And rise the morning day

Let the age die and burn around me

Another way—have I

To see clarity beyond the stars

From in the upper room

It blazes fire on Misery's Train

A harbinger of doom

840

Out in the barn—in an evil that no one soul can name

Live spiders shadowing all normal tarantulas to shame

Single orbs weaved from wooden beams all the way down to the floor

Enormous creatures in a row made of no less than three or four

Gigantic webs made perpendicular to the straw across the floor—

Lightning fear—down to the core!

Bodies girthed to the tallness and to the width of average man

Legs far above and beyond the height of every human span

Promises of a death delivered for what recompense is due

A nightmare of pain delivered over and beyond what is overdue

A trembling quivered from the head and from the heart down to the shoe—

'Tis Satan—to me and you!

Jonathan Lovejoy

841

He directs in the power of destiny

Motivation is key

Laziness sings a swan song

Industry makes a call

Left stranded in downtown nowhere

Nothing—caretaker of

Man's dominion over creation is out

Subjugation is in

Eat cake to enjoy the sweetness

Appreciate the skill

Old desperation is new again

Coming over the hill

Improvements often come to naught

Original is best

Inspiration is fleeting—like a bird

A fledgling in the nest

Elizabethan VI

Stay true to thine calling—
Whatever it may be
It will pay off in due time
Beyond what you can see

842

*Y*our doors and windows must be shut

Or at least—a screen

Unless precaution is gravely shown

A monkey might get in

Screeching—running through the house

Tearing it asunder

While the owner of it stands idly by

As though he can do nothing

The flowers can provide no beauty

Scattered across the lawn

While the monkey is somewhere in the house

A demon in the dark

177th Assembly

843

I desire things that can never be—
Are they nature, or sin?
Is there difference between the two?
Praise to Golgotha, then!

The Spirit is willing—the flesh is weak
When weariness sets in
By only this station—Almighty God
O'er temptation we win

844

Seclusion is not secular—
As inclusion is
Reclusion comes Divine—
By direction—His

She is my desperation
Without knowing why
Gathers my affection—
Her discerning eye

Jonathan Lovejoy

845

Take a trip down Abbey Road

Where four geniuses live

Watch them earn their comeuppances

With no more lives to give—

One—Intellectualism

Two—Creativity

Three—Spiritualism

Four—Tranquility

A jam session with them is not desirable

Seeing as they are dead

Have no part of the Golden Apple

To thine own fruits instead

846

I should like to gaze upon the body—

She was in

To touch it—

To feel it—

To carry it to my dying day

In the hope that who she was—

Is a part of me

Jonathan Lovejoy

178th Assembly

847

Discourse sings adagio

His sermon is the storm

Upon conclusion of andante

Con Brio is the norm

Allegro's Flame fires at will

To ashes they will burn

No further complications rise

Nor lessons left to learn

Elizabethan VI

848

I was struck by the beauty of the contestant

As we prepared the game

With loving care and whole heartedness

Yet frightened all the same

849

On the nighttime sands to nowhere
In the aftermath of rolling tide
Disillusionment drifts upon a fog
To cover the sands of time

Lightning fear abounds
In the morning hour
Without the break of dawn
To light a dreary path

850

I builded the tower unawares
From the bottom to the sky
I asked myself—what madness is this—
But never knowing why

Thou accursed foundation hath been blessed
To future heights unknown
The Tower reaches toward the Heavens
Builded by blood and bone

179th Assembly

851

In back of the Great Music Hall
A Holy Sign appears
Speaking of days that have come and gone—
And those that soon will be

Get it right the second time—
The fire must be reborn!
Flames of crimson and amber stock
Burning yellow and red

Who can be trusted to correct the flame—
Among the worthy elite?
Destiny guides the willing hand
Through the task it must complete

852

"*Have you accepted Jesus as your Lord and Savior?*"

Be not afraid to ask

Shelly was 18—when they scraped her off the road

Drunk driving was the task

Come back to my weeping bed, Mother Dear!

Ask Christ to save my soul

When they pulled Shelly's body off the highway

No one had played the role!

What if Christianity is true?

Our faith can never tell

Whether or not Shelly went to Heaven

Or if she burns in Hell

853

*B*eauty decorates the salvage yard

Hope to a dying day

The Janet Bird hath flown the coop

I longed for her to stay!

854

She looked through a so-called Christian hole

A demon came up through it—

A portal to the pits of—

There's no need to pursue it!

180th Assembly

Jonathan Lovejoy

855

In the House of Perpetuity—they drift

Spirits of another Time

Seeking forgiveness for the pain they caused

In another life

One who writhes in Poverty

The other—

In the torment of Death

856

Success will find no home

Through Desperation's door

The House of Poverty—joy and laughter

Ghosts they are striving for

857

*T*he name carves an imposing figure
Across the art display
Reducing others to none effect
With little more to say

Those who seek to sabotage
Do so without regret
Spreading false colors across the art—
With neither fit nor fret!

Gatekeepers are poisoned with envy—
So sings the clarinet!

858

I desire no new life—

Except for one I know

To live as to the Will of God—

Then off to Heaven we go!

181st Assembly

859

She knows exactly how it feels, like floating in the sky

Through the straw and up her nose, it sings a lullabye

You can say goodnight to sanity, my Princess Diamond Vy

At the funeral your mother will scream to God and ask him why

When they put you in the ground she'll scream to God and Christ—oh why!

Why Oh Lord, did she have to die?

860

I probe the dark, witchy side of come hither
Waiting to be born
I have no reason to live, Anathema—

 Dictionary does no good

Fettertwelp and hot stove memories

Harkle down the whisper trail

With corncob pipes and button noses

Burning through the snow

I'm not at all—there's no oil this month

Fearlessly clean in the dictaroot

Wild parties chase the rabbit

Down the hole until he is found Weezle—

Thy wicked hands abound!

Nothing's ever been played before—

Until now

Dweeped in the dwittle

Find out about the kittle

Ask Miss Mittle—

If she wants to come, too

There's room for one more!

All in all, elevator goes back two floors—

Imagine that!

Old is made new

And new is old again

Lack of Claire (clarity) is frustrating

Is she not?

Almost every time I've learned to say goodbye—

It happens

861

Listen to the angel and demon parade

They contain truths to hear

Things about yourself you don't want to face

Changes within the year

Somewhere in the Parade of Spirits

Truth you're destined to know

Cutting painfully to the core—

Making you long for Death

Outside the Castle of Pipe Dreams

The Parade walks idly by

Looking to lay agonizing truth—

Making you pray to die

862

Put her in the bowels of Earth

And let it ease your mind

See your grief churn the spinning day

Her coffin—intertwined

182nd Assembly

863

There is a war that rages—
Between the heart and the mind
When the mind wishes to think good things
The heart becomes a whirlwind

A vortex of human nature
Pulling, luring—like a body in space
Drawing objects in around it—
Or smashing them to oblivion
On the surface of desire

And there are times when the reverse is true
When the heart desireth to do good
To dwell upon things that are right—
And pure
But the mind is suddenly wicked and corrupt
As the evil heart had been

Elizabethan VI

This battle rages—

Over the soil of human nature

Where the seeds of goodness are planted Only to be choked in the

Garden of Weeds The battlefield of good versus evi

The war between the flesh—

And the spirit

Jonathan Lovejoy

864

_L_ove—cherish thy thought

As rain

From Heaven above—

Perish thy miseries wrought

865

Humor Life to his Demand
Though he gives no return
Turn the other cheek—says so
Deny thy passions—burn!

Birth carries no pretense to good
From Cradle—to thy Grave
Cry no tears for me—Dear Heart
Thine only soul to save!

Lightning sparks the bluest flame
 In the eve—a drowning rain
Life in Thunder's mocking word
Awake! Receive thy pain!

866

A trip through this Atramental Wood

Creatures both great and small

Crawl me into accursed fright—

Unmerciful at all!

183rd Assembly

867

I never met a verse by her

That left me well alone

That did not set my soul afire

Or chill me to the bone

Her axe wields of Divine Order—

A chisel into stone

868

A stroll in the field of souls
Shows others dressed in white
Ignorant of what curse or calling
Was given in the night

Striding the campus of lost dreams
Wanting life to begin
Who among the blessed—or accursed few
Is in the hell I'm in?

869

*T*he pages of this book are torn
The cover is spotted—dark—

Frayed around the edges
It is not a book whose cover invites

Inside may be purest inspiration

Wisdom from on high—

True Inspiration is one percent Knowledge

And ninety nine percent Imagination

The kind that is divine in origin

That leads to Revelation—

And Truth

For though they never saw the Garden

Nor the Fall of Man

Nor the Great Flood—

They knew

Elizabethan VI

870

Sleep is my best friend
Waking is to dread
Repose is medicine for an ill

Darkness is my bed

A breeze—to wrap a soul to ice

Tremble at what it said!

184th Assembly

Jonathan Lovejoy

871

The Cronus Butterfly has curious properties

It has no defenses
No protection against the elements
No shelter from the wind
Save one—

When there is a season of turmoil
The Cronus Butterfly freezes itself immobile
Outside the flow of time
There it hangs in mid air
Invulnerable—

An untouchable swallowtail of beauty
It waits for the deadly season to pass
Before it phases into time again
For this reason—

872

*C*ronus appears as a Butterfly

To mark the flow of time
Freezing immobile during flight—
In jaded wing sublime

Of being born into this world
A creature of free will
Fluttering the Earth in fear and dread
Waiting for us to kill

Who would harm the Cronus Butterfly?
Believe the legend, still

873

*O*ver analysis tends to corrupt
Any fair view of the moment
Tis best to look in with the heart
Rather than the mind—

Where other values are obtained
Perfect order is simply gained

874

O Winter—

Let thy accusations in!

Allow thy storm of grief to blow
Shivering me to the bone
Show fervent anger in the snow
Let grief and violence moan

Howl thy displeasure to the world at large
Across the Winter windswept Earth
Through thy fallen flakes of snow
Let avarice be known

What corner of the Earth—what pocket of the world
Doth this cloude abide?
From where above the seeded plain Comes
forth this grain of snow?

875

Waiting to be alive

Demure—these gutters

Futile uncertainty—flutters in the breeze

Occasionally shudders

No pathetic ribbon—

Thy grieving bed is laid—

Now lie in it!

185th Assembly

876

*K*now this—father!

While you strike fire into your child's skin
While you draw blood from his veins
That what goes around—
Comes mightily around again

Mother! Know this! While you stand
idly by
That thine own comeuppance is gravely due
From thy Queen's Crown
To the sole of thy feet—
Thou divinest comeuppance is overdue!

I curse the witch who bore me!
I spit on the grave of the devil who beat me sore!

877

Signs of failure continue to show

In the fall of Future's Night

Names printed ineffectually

Evening tasks left undone

On the ebony canvas

A crimson lie appears

Reappearing on the night ground

In red line form

Beside the cropfield of delusion

Fruitless labour beckons

To imprison an unsuspecting fool

In a living death

878

C lose the book on silly dreams

And look at the real world

For what purpose can a blue sunrise be—

What privilege doth a purple tree provide?

Listen to the real world breeze

Blowing over leaves of jaded green

Watch the sunset with waking eyes

To see whether it be amber

879

O fear!

Touch my shoulder!
Let me know that I am alive—
And breathing

O Lord!
Cast my dreary day—
To the Bright Land Sea

Fear keeps a claw in my back
My head
My heart
Threatening a talon to squeeze

To pierce me
To carry me off as prey

186th Assembly

880

Take pleasure in the royal hand

It was given for thee

Skin as smooth as spun silk

A heart strung as the violin

Skills mastered by a blessed few

Can charm the heart of a queen

881

I should like to guest at the Homestead

Alas—am I able?

Trembling—a mountain of it lies

As their flight—to Egypt

Blessed Virgin—for where to rest

Alas— 'cept thy stable

Spirit of Bethlehem—above

Amherst Descends the Lamb of God

882

There is a level of poverty in the world

We do not want to know

Where horror stories are a daily thing

Too terrible to show

Overseas charity can be a rouge

Do we make ourselves clear?

Hypocrisy on an epic scale

Year after blessed year

What will we do if someday—

Destiny finds a cure

Where will the Charity Yacht, Christine?

Park its pristine allure?

883

Endeavor for death to find me
With no pain or fear
Hear the voice of the archangel
Hearken unto him

If he saith—"thou shalt not die"
Disobey thy whim
To stroll Dissolution's Forest Wood—
Heed no falling limb!

Jonathan Lovejoy

Jonathan Lovejoy

187th Assembly

Jonathan Lovejoy

884

If not a jail of bars and doors

A prison of the mind

It happens through the mother line

Regardless of the crime

885

A fire blazes through the kitchen
Flames of amber and white
Threatening to melt Creation
And everything in sight

The fire burns hottest unsuspected
Flames appear first undetected
In white and amber light

886

I know—in times like this

She feels the most motherly

What has she done—what has qualified her

For this Great Honor?

That which can idea—

From "Debonair"

Walking the streets of this paradise

Is a swim in shark infested waters

Where the sharks are gangs

Drug dealers—

And the like

Elizabethan VI

887

She plays a conscious bay
Piano—geeked at individuals
Whose interest is piqued by the keyboard
That plays here all alone

Jessica on the keys is a sight to see
Those in the know go to bended knee
Whenever her face is shown

Jonathan Lovejoy

188th Assembly

888

"Ah, look at all the lonely people"
Said the Music Man to me
Concerning souls adrift—to and fro
Church of the Nativity

They roam o'er sea to shining sea
Painful loss of Divinity
A grieving Home to be

889

Not every calling is nobility

Or greatness—born

Some wander without a home

Ballast—forlorn

No respector of persons, His

The Wealth of Kings

As too, the Curse of Poverty

Thy mourning rings

Jonathan Lovejoy

890

If thou shalt bear false witness
God will brand thee—"Liar"
Poised to take thy rightful place
Beside the Lake of Fire

Sing this warning for the people
Ring the bell, church tower steeple
Humanity's desire

891

If happiness should bear a call
Bid a formal greeting
Stroll with her a garden mile
Fleeting—begs her pardon

Footsteps toward the Promised Land
Joy and Sorrow—hand in hand
A resting ground to harden

189th Assembly

892

Take a trip to the outer banks
Give sorrow to the wave

Let them carry it out to sea

Bless thy watery grave

In the surf—the sounding sea

Rolling voice of Eternity

Immortal soul to save

Elizabethan VI

893

Lend no thought to the Spirit World

What purpose can it be?

Let the Spirits roam undisturbed

Beyond where eyes can see

By Them, ourselves doth intertwine

This road of life, His Will Divine

By Him—the Golden Key

Jonathan Lovejoy

894

Laugh away a strange woman
Open—if you dare
Your heart to run away from her
Privilege—unaware

Malls, markups, Birkenstocks
What is it that they know?
Shoes, socks, Mantleclocks
More merchandise to show

Prayers prayed in hypocrisy
Heroes guilty as sin
One hundred yards is as a hundred years
For all travelers therin

Underneath skies of apocalypse
Pockets of innocence
Protected by the Hand of God
Days of no repentance

Elizabethan VI

On the streets of Perpetuity
"Michael" runs to and fro
Bodies broken by Destiny
The Pain of Life to know

Jonathan Lovejoy

895

The piano is the key

Played by a lack of skill

Covering the world in dissonance

While hope has come to naught

Those with greater ability

Look onward with disdain

No pity for the Loser's Pain

With nothing more to gain

Search the ground for the yellow bird

Hidden among the brush

The number commissioned with is 5

Rush in the grass to take—

Fake birds do threaten a call

A painted yellow dove

A journey filled with false symbols

Commissioned from above

190th Assembly

Jonathan Lovejoy

896

Would she be happier as a clam

On Eternity's beach?

Would she be happier on a tram

Eating a Georgia peach?

Would she be happier on the lam

From Reality's reach

897

A comedy is in the balance
And waits there all alone
Sister Sue is on the phone
Waiting for what she needs!

Behind the walls of Amherst
Suspicions do abound
Was she verbally abused
Mistreated like a hound?

Shunned by the world she lived in
Save her grieving bed
Strength by the Angel of the Lord
The Bride of Christ to wed

898

As Want retreats behind the mist
Like unto silvery sheen
Bordered on the Bed of Rose
Then off to Abilene

Her thoughts dispersed as phantom smoke
With nothing in between
Though substance weighs a heavy mountain
Her slopes of Appenine

899

Eyes of blue

Eyes of gray

Eyes of day and night

Satan's eyes will make you obey

The longing for a flight

From the ghost world, cool breezes blow

Lifting the soul with no desire

For such a dreadful fright

191ˢᵗ Assembly

Jonathan Lovejoy

900

Isolation is idealism for most

Reality—for some

They inhabit a prison without walls

In grieving for a home

901

*L*ook to the North for guidance

There, you'll see a star

Shining brightness from afar

To immortality—sail onward—Dearest!

You'll never be alone

The Glory of the Lord is shown

A heartsick flow of verse from thee

Regret for daily living—

Bestowed to a heart of giving

When the sun rises in the East

Life's purpose is known to thee

Beyond where the eye can see

Jonathan Lovejoy

902

White explosions in the sky
Against the sea of blue

Rolling, billowing clouds of might

At the foot of the Throne of God

Towering mountains of snowy white

Angels above the Earth

Aglow of the power Silvery Bright

Delight in the hour of men

903

Yellow roses sing a lullaby
Across a crowded room

Even in playces where Spirits roam
And prophecies of doom

"Gregory" sees one at the window
Inside the dark'ned hall
Causing him to run for his life
With no concern at all—

For my feeble explanation
Boy, it was just a dream
Its only a white light in the window
Gauging you for a scream!

192nd Assembly

904

The road to success is perilous
For them who seek to gain
Wrought with dead ends and pitfalls
Inducive to defeat

Traveling along the road of life
Minding my own affairs
The road was suddenly blocked by water
Shocking me unawares

In the Halls of Perpetuity
The ancestry requires
Generosity for a useless thing
Envious desires

Wedded to elusive success
Her timeline begs to own
The gates of Hell cannot prevent
A calling from His throne

905

Death is my constant companion

At first far off, so near

I should like to have a talk with him

'Til his gray voice is clear

Bear no thought of me, he said

Thy feeble heart be grudged

For it is appointed once to die

Then after this, be judged!

Then he said, Farewell to thee

I saw him travel on

And though I cannot find him—still—

His voice is never gone

906

Beware of too much ability

Doing less good, than harm

Facility—without depth of thought

May hold no depth of charm

907

Pain will cause the stress of life

Tensions—builded up

Except thy pressure be relieved

There will a break occur

Upon this crumbling, grieving heart

Devastation flew

Leaving the nerves a pile of rubble

With miseries—anew

Jonathan Lovejoy

193rd Assembly

Jonathan Lovejoy

908

Of the newest "daguerreotype"

'Tis very likely she

Proof may be the evil eye

In the Face of Death

Science cannot find her

Neither geometry

This latter-day ghost must be *reversed*

So modern eyes can see

909

Ride the bus to frivolity   They are beauty—times five

Although worldiness doth abound

At least—their kind and good heart is found

Strolling through the Land of Knee Hoping to stay alive

A timid knock on every door To find who it is I'm looking for

I rode the bus to frivolity

They were beauty—times five

Now, there are no more of them

To help me stay alive

910

Would that my time among the populace

Were as amidst the trees

Ode to serenity--peaceful nature

Flutters along the breeze

How it doth please summer's voice to carry

The Meadowlark's Reprise

911

I gathered the rights to four generations

To carry on a stroll

Across the windswept countryside

Of the Grieving Land

The sun shines over the prairie plain

In the heat of solemn renewel

In a crystal clear blue sky above

Down to every horizon

Entrusted with a sacred scroll

To carry on the Word

On the rise of worldwide immorality

And the fall of innocence

A stroll across the nighttime Grieving Land

To the amaranthine flow

Reveals a rendezvous with good fortune

And blessings overdue

Jonathan Lovejoy

The Fall of the Music Man is key
A sign for the closing age
In the calm before the approaching storm
Of eschatology

194th Assembly

Jonathan Lovejoy

912

Inspiration bares her fleeting heart

Thy Muse—a fickled thing

There hath been not a fledgling born

Inspired to take wing

Time brings compassion upon the soul

Who desireth to sing

913

It would seem that "flambé" has returned

To compound the sorrows of mankind

While seeking to gain from lost ability

Fools of wrath go stumbling blind

Through the gray world of lost expectations

 In the land of broken and shattered dreams

Those who are in the know don't know

The consequences of their Earthen schemes

The violent color is trauma unbridled

Leading only to defeat

The selling point for grits is butter—

Among the privileged and the worthy elite

914

Trouble looms above the horizon

Body or spirit harm

Naught to do but pray away

Leave prosperity rule the day

Hold thy poverty and despair at bay

Withold my soul's alarm!

Dissolution surveys fallen leaves

Across the fertile ground

Trouble lurks among Autumn Trees

Piercing eyes to our soul with ease

In grief to devour what manner they please

For my burial ground

915

Among the forest trees of autumn
Disillusionment scatters the weary ground
As those who despise look on in mocking
Craving my defeat

In the Halls of Pergatory
Between poverty and prosperity
Hatred manifests in armistice
To remove the innocent to prison

A malicious spirit haunts the ancestry
Causing a craving for mischief
While signs of trouble sear upon the coals
Beneath the pauper's table

Ghosts hide in every closet
Waiting for me to come in
To be thrown inside by the mother line
And left there in the dark

916

Old sins do come a knockin'
Threatening anew
Cold winds have come a rockin'
Reddening to blue

ABOUT THE AUTHOR

Jonathan Lovejoy is a graduate of the University of North Carolina at Greensboro, with a B.A. in Religious Studies. He currently lives in Winston Salem, North Carolina.

For more info on the author's life and career, visit jonathanlovejoy.com.